Dreamjob

A play

Graham Jones

Samuel French - London
New York - Toronto - Hollywood

ISBN 0 573 03379 X

Please see page iv for further copyright information

CHARACTERS

Angela
Joan
Mandy
Beverly
Fiona

The action takes place in a waiting-room

Time—the present

(See also page ii)

DREAMJOBS

A bare stage except for six chairs in a row and a closed door at the end of the row

Sitting on the chair nearest the door is Angela, legs crossed, filing her nails, chewing gum. She is about fifteen years old, fairly attractive but a trifle coarse in manners and behaviour. She has a habit of sniffing occasionally

After a while Joan enters and walks towards the row of chairs. She is not so coarse as Angela, rather more sensitive by nature, well groomed, better dressed than Angela, good-looking but not in any obvious way sexy. She does not sit down for a while, but looks at Angela, who glances up from perusal of her fingernails. Joan smiles, but the smile is not returned. Angela looks back at her fingernails

Angela You too!
Joan Yes.

Joan takes a seat—a seat not too close to Angela

Angela Wait here all day.
Joan What do we do? Just sit here?
Angela What else?
Joan Should we knock?
Angela I have already. There's no-one there yet. (*Pause*) Where's your friend?
Joan Who?
Angela 'Ent she coming?
Joan Mandy?
Angela The one who's always with you.
Joan Yes: Mandy.
Angela The one who's always on about being an air hostess. (*She sniggers*) Air hostess!
Joan (*timidly*) Well, I don't see anything wrong with that . . .
Angela Don't you?
Joan No.
Angela (*sarcastically*) Air hostess!

Joan (*uncertainly*) Well . . .
Angela Well, what?
Joan She could.
Angela Never.
Joan She might.
Angela Not ever. Not her.

A silence

Joan How long've you been here?
Angela Ages. Days!
Joan And nobody's come?
Angela They'll just keep you waiting hours. Having a cup of tea somewhere, I 'spect. Anyway, it's better here than lessons. Better than Fanny Price any day of the week, the bitch.
Joan What's she done?
Angela Nothin'. Why?
Joan (*timidly*) Just wondered . . .
Angela Wha'?
Joan Calling her a bitch.
Angela I called her that because that's what she is and always have been; ever since she started trying to teach me English. (*Under her breath*) Just because I can't spell very well.
Joan What?
Angela Nothin'.

Mandy comes in. She is about the same age as the other two, slightly podgy but not unattractive: a little bit of a snob, quite well-spoken. She and Joan are close friends

Mandy Where've you been? I thought you were waiting for me, Joan.
Joan I came on down. I told you . . .
Mandy But I thought you were waiting *there.*

Mandy glances at Angela, and Angela, as it were, sniffs recognition

Angela Who wants to spell words anyway?

Mandy looks a little bemused and looks questioningly at Joan

Hankerchief. (*Spelling it out*) H.A.N.K.E.R.C.H.E.E.F. (*Imitating Miss Price*) "There's a D in hankerchief. HandDkerchief." Who cares? (*She sniffs and wipes her sleeve across her nose*) Who uses 'em anyway?

Mandy (*to Joan*) She going on about Miss Price again?

Angela Wha's 'at?

Mandy Just wondering if you were going on about Miss Price again.

Angela (*scornfully*) *Miss* Price! You mean Fanny Price.

Mandy sits down next to Joan and talks intimately to her: Angela listens

Mandy Remember what I was telling you about the B.O.A.C., Joan?

Joan Yes.

Mandy Well, my father rung them up yesterday.

Joan looks suitably impressed

And they said that if I could pass a certain test which they set, and then go for an interview and pass that, then . . .

Angela (*ironically*) You could fly!

Mandy turns to look at Angela but Angela is inspecting her finger-nails, so Mandy turns back to speak to Joan

Mandy I could become an air hostess.

Joan That's good, Mandy. Do you think you'll pass?

Mandy I think I'll be all right in the interview—do my best anyway—but I'm not so sure with the written exam. (*She sighs*) It's what I want to do more than anything, Joan.

Joan Yes.

Angela sniffs loudly. They both look at her

Angela You wouldn't catch me dead in one of them things—them aeroplanes. They're always crashing.

Mandy (*as if from a brochure*) They're the safest form of transport there is.

Angela There's one or two of them down in flames every day. Then there's hi-jacks.

Mandy does not quite know what to say: she shuffles uncomfortably and a little irritably in her seat

D'you know what I'd wish? I'd wish to see Fanny Price get a job as a air hostess, that's what I'd wish.

Angela smiles to herself. Mandy gives Joan a "tut tut" sort of look

Mandy (*more quietly*) The man on the phone said that if my application was put in soon . . .
Angela It 'ent much of a job.
Mandy What isn't?
Angela Air hostess.
Mandy It is.
Angela That's a matter of opinion, 'ent it?

Beverly enters. She is tall, attractive, looks a good deal older than her fifteen years. She exudes confidence and is a little arrogant. She likes herself, knows she is attractive and tends to pose when she stands to speak. She is quite friendly with Angela who admires her: she does not pay much attention to the other two

Beverly What's a matter of opinion?
Angela Her—she thinks being an air hostess is everything.

Beverly deigns to glance in Mandy's direction

Beverly Who wants to serve drinks all day?
Mandy You don't have to. There's other things too . . .
Angela Such as?
Mandy Such as . . .
Beverly "Fasten your seat belts, please."

Angela laughs raucously

Mandy You don't know anything about it.
Beverly How long've we got to wait here, for crying out loud?

Angela shrugs her shoulders. Beverly stands with a hand on her hip, her head thrown slightly back, one foot crossed over the other

(*pointing to the door*) If they don't find me something to do with what I'm cut out for, I'll tell them just what they can do with their Youth Employment Service.
Mandy And what are you supposed to be cut out for?

Beverly does a twirl and a few steps of a dance

Joan Dancing's not a job.

Beverly glances at Joan contemptuously

Beverly (*to Mandy*) What's *she* doing here? The way she talks, you'd think she never wanted a job.
Angela Who does?
Beverly Me. I want to dance.

She snaps her fingers rhythmically. After a while Angela too snaps her fingers rhythmically. Angela stands up and together with Beverly they perform a few dance steps

Joan (*standing up*) It's not a job. Dancing's not a job.

But Angela and Beverly are not listening. Again they begin snapping their fingers, only this time dance music is heard, at first faintly but gradually increasing in intensity. The atmosphere changes gradually: lights change in colour; spotted lights flash around the room as if they are in a dance hall. Beverly is dreaming. The others have to take part in her dream whether they like it or not. They all dance in a group for a while, then they are "choreographed" back into their former positions before the dance began

Fiona enters. She is a plump dumpling of a girl who tends to take things rather seriously though she is a little fussy

Fiona Wha' was all that?
Beverly What?
Fiona That racket.

They all look at each other queerly

Thought I heard music.
Beverly You must have been dreaming.

Fiona shrugs her shoulders and takes a seat

Fiona (*to Joan*) Anybody about here? You been seen yet?
Joan No. Just waiting.
Fiona (*to everybody*) Anybody been seen yet?

They tell her "No"

Some school this is: they tell us to be here on time and then nothing. (*She looks closely at Joan*) You all right, Joan?
Joan Yes. Why?
Fiona You look a bit pale, that's all.
Joan I'm all right.

Fiona gets up, walks briskly to the door and raps on it. No reply, so she resumes her seat. Angela winks at Beverly

Angela (*to Fiona*) How's Geoff?
Fiona Shurrup.
Beverly (*to Angela*) Wha' Geoff?
Angela Geoff Millar, 'course.

Mandy looks "daggers" at Angela and Beverly. Joan looks upset

Beverly (*shrieking*) Geoff Millar!
Fiona Shurrup.
Beverly Geoff Millar!
Angela He's nice, 'en't he, Fiona?
Fiona How would I know?
Beverly Geoff Millar!
Mandy (*standing up*) Why keep saying his name?
Beverly (*laughing*) I don't know. It's just that I didn't know about them: Geoff and Fiona.
Fiona I don't know him. Anyway, he's a pig.

A silence

Joan He's not.
Fiona I don't know if he is or not. I don't even know him, so there.
Joan (*upset*) He's not a pig.
Beverly Geoff Millar and Fiona!
Joan (*angrily*) What's wrong with that?
Beverly I don't know, I'm sure. (*She sniggers*) How should I know anything about him? I've never been out with him.
Mandy Perhaps he's never asked.
Beverly Oh, he's asked, all right. He's always asking. He asks everybody. And anybody who's daft enough to go out with him gets what she deserves . . .
Joan Leave her alone.
Beverly Who?
Joan Fiona.

Fiona is a little bemused

Beverly What have I said? All I said was that Geoff Millar . . .
Joan Well, don't keep saying it.

Beverly Why not? I can say "Geoff Millar" as many times as I like. Geoff Millar, Geoff Millar . . .

Joan bursts into tears and sits down. Mandy confronts Beverly

Mandy There's no need for you to go on about it, is there?
Beverly About what?
Mandy You know what.

Beverly makes a face and looks at Angela

Angela (*in a stage whisper*) Her and him.
Beverly Who and who? (*Surprised*) Joan and Geoff? No—they're not!
Mandy So why don't you leave her alone?

Beverly is surprised and a little sorry but Mandy's remark makes her put on an attitude of not caring

Beverly I've left her alone, don't worry. And you too. You *and* your aeroplanes!

Beverly sits down and crosses her legs and poses as usual. Mandy returns to comfort Joan

Mandy (*to Joan*) Don't worry, Joan. She's just ignorant, she is. She hasn't got feelings about things.
Beverly (*singing quietly*) "She flies like a bird in the sky-y-y-y."

Angela laughs. Beverly gets up and goes around the room with arms outstretched like an aeroplane. Angela and Fiona laugh and team up behind her

It's climbing, it's climbing, higher and higher . . .

They make the noise of the engines. Mandy is transported to her dream world. The atmosphere in the room changes: the roar of the engines becomes a real roar on tape. The girls arrange the chairs so that they appear to be rows of seats in an aeroplane. Mandy buttons up her coat so that it looks like an air hostess's uniform and she walks briskly, importantly, to the back of the row and then walks slowly down the aisle between the chairs in which the girls, as passengers, are now sitting

Mandy (*to Angela*) Everything all right, madam?
Angela Can I unfasten my safety belt now?

Mandy Certainly, madam—we've stopped climbing now. Perhaps you'd like to look out of the window at the view of the coastline.

Angela What time will we arrive in Spain?

Mandy First we stop at Perpignan, then cross into Northern Spain and arrive at Barcelona at approximately two o'clock, madam.

Angela Thank you—you're so kind.

Mandy moves on to the next person

Mandy Anything I can get you, madam?

Beverly Yes, please: a John Collins mixed with—let me see—a Coke. On the rocks. In a tall glass. With a straw.

Mandy makes notes on an invisible pad and moves on

Mandy Everything all right, madam?

Joan I'm not feeling too well.

Mandy Shall I get you a glass of water?

Joan You see, I'm going to have a baby.

Fiona (*looking around*) I'm a nurse.

Mandy (*to Fiona, sharply*) If you don't mind, I'll take care of the young lady.

Fiona But I'm a qualified nurse. Perhaps she'd like an aspirin.

Mandy If you don't mind, miss, I'm the air hostess. (*To Joan*) Now, if you'll keep perfectly calm then everything will be all right.

She holds her hand for a while until Joan drops off to sleep. Mandy moves on to Fiona. She is a trifle peeved with her

Anything I can get *you*, miss?

Fiona Yes, please. You can get me—let me see—you can get me . . .

Mandy Yes?

Fiona The pilot. When we land, please.

The lights change and everything is back to normal

Mandy You've spoilt it now. It's always spoilt.

Fiona Or before we land, if you like—I don't mind either way.

Mandy It's spoilt.

The others move the chairs back to where they were before the dream. Mandy goes over to sit by Joan, who is whimpering

Don't worry, Joan.
Joan How can I help worrying? There's my parents to think about. If only he liked me now but he just ignores me, he just hates me now.
Mandy No, he doesn't.
Joan But he does, Mandy, he does.
Mandy You'll have to tell him.

A silence

He doesn't already know!
Joan Yes.
Mandy What did he say when you told him?
Joan Nothing.
Mandy Nothing!
Joan Nothing. Just shrugged his shoulders.
Mandy But if he's responsible then . . .
Joan What?
Mandy Then . . .
Joan Then nothing.

They both become grimly silent. Fiona walks over to Angela and Beverly

Fiona Miss Price see you about your work?
Angela (*scornfully*) Miss Price! Fanny Price. Who cares about her anyway?
Fiona I had to do mine all over because I couldn't spell five words. "Persuasion" was one, and . . .
Angela Persuasion? What did you want to use a word like that for anyway?
Fiona Can't remember. Then there was "their". I put "there". (*She spells it out*)
Angela Who cares? Their—there—same thing. Fanny Price!
Fiona I care. Well, I do. I've got to get "O" level English to be a nurse.
Angela Fanny Price caught me out on "handkerchief", the bitch.
Beverly A nurse! Some job!
Angela Terrible uniforms. Like bats flying around in them cloaks.

Beverly Terrible hours: nights, days, work, work, work, forty-eight hours a day.
Angela And the rest!
Beverly And the blood!
Angela And bed-pans!
Fiona (*eagerly*) And doctors.

As Fiona goes starry-eyed, the atmosphere in the room changes again. This time the familiar signature tune of a television series on hospitals is heard: then the sound of an ambulance siren. Chairs are moved into line to simulate an operating-bed. Beverly becomes the surgeon, Angela becomes the patient on the bed. Fiona is, of course, the nurse. Joan and Mandy are "lesser" nurses. Beverly proceeds to tap bones, take the patient's pulse, listen to her heart, etc.

Beverly I'm afraid we are too late, Nurse—the patient is dying.
Fiona Shall I get a bed pan, Doctor?

Angela looks up. Beverly gives Fiona a sort of "give up?" look

Beverly Scalpel, please, Nurse.
Fiona (*pretending to hand it to her*) Scalpel, Doctor.
Beverly Forceps, Nurse.
Fiona Forceps, Doctor.
Beverly Now you two juniors—

Fiona gives them a "snooty" look

—if you will just hold the patient down while I—while I . . . (*She loses her nerve suddenly*) I can't do it. I can't go through with it.
Fiona But, Doctor, you must. Try to pull yourself together. You've done thousands of operations like this before, Doctor, so why do you hesitate now?
Beverly Because, Nurse—the patient—is my own daughter.
Fiona I see.
Joan (*in a panic*) What can we do, Nurse?
Mandy Shall I see if there is another surgeon available?
Fiona No time. There's only one thing *to* do. I myself will have to proceed with the operation.

Angela opens her eyes and looks up, and swallows hard

Joan But Nurse, you can't . . .
Fiona No "buts", please. Scalpel.
Joan Scalpel.
Fiona Forceps.
Joan Forceps.
Fiona (*falteringly*) Er—yes, let me see—bed-pan.

The girls throw their arms up in despair and the spell of the dream is broken. They return the chairs to their former positions as they talk

Beverly Fine nurse you'd make. They'd be dying off like flies.
Fiona Well, they wouldn't, so there. I'd make a good nurse.
Beverly You talk as if that's what you're going to be—as if that's what they're going to advise you in there. You won't ever be a nurse, Fiona. Not in a million years.

Fiona looks depressed. A silence. Beverly looks at Fiona and feels sorry that she said what she did. She too looks a bit depressed

I wonder if any of us will ever be what we want to be.

Beverly glances across at Joan, then gets up and goes over to sit next to her

I'm sorry about what I said.
Joan That's all right. You didn't say anything very much.
Beverly He's no good. You know that, don't you? (*No reply*) Geoff Millar! (*Pause*) Do your parents know?

Joan shakes her head

Is it too late to . . .?
Joan Yes.
Beverly Better tell them then.
Joan My father'll kill me.
Beverly Men! (*She stands up*) I'll never know what I see in them. (*She strolls over to the door*) Haven't they finished their tea yet? Angela, knock on the door and tell them you've been here for three days and that you want to put your name down for—(*looking at her*)—for what?
Angela Modelling.
Fiona You're not!
Angela Why not?

Fiona (*embarrassedly*) No reason. Just that . . . Well—I thought you had to be about six feet tall.

Beverly You're tall enough, aren't you, Ang? Stand up, Angela: let's see what you're like for a model.

Angela stands up and walks to the far end of the row of chairs. As Beverly begins to speak so the atmosphere in the room changes again: soft lights, sweet music. Angela walks forward in the way models walk in fashion parades

Here we have Angela in a long, flowing dress suitable for evening parties or visits to Buckingham Palace and such like places. Take particular notice of the fine waistline and the cut of the shoulders—how subtly it follows the contours of Angela's figure. Made from the finest of silks, costing only five hundred pounds. Ladies and gentlemen—Angela.

Angela returns to the back of the row and begins to walk again. This time Mandy does the commentary

Mandy Angela again, ladies and gentlemen: this time in a close-fitting outfit made of satin, in a soothing shade of green, very much resembling the superb uniform worn by B.O.A.C. air hostesses. Note the cut of the jacket and the bold line of the skirt, costing a mere six hundred and fifty pounds. I give you Angela.

Now Joan speaks as Angela models

Joan Here she is again in a loose-fitting outfit, suitable for all occasions. Please notice that it can also be worn by the larger lady or for the woman who is soon expecting to have a baby. Ladies and gentlemen—Angela.

Lastly Fiona speaks

Fiona Angela again, everyone, this time in an off-the-shoulder very, very revealing sexy outfit that shows just about all she's got—and more!

Angela gives a "look"

And a mini skirt high enough to reveal her stocking tops and a buttonless jacket which opens wide to reveal . . .

Angela Oh, for heaven's sake, Fiona!

Fiona What have I done now?

The dream spell is broken

Angela (*to Fiona*) You spoil everything.
Fiona I do my best.
Beverly Well, your best just isn't good enough then.
Fiona (*sulkily*) I can't help it if I'm no good at things, can I?

They all sit down and look rather fed up

Beverly No, Fiona, you can't help it. (*Pause*) None of us can.
Mandy What?
Beverly Help it. Help ourselves. Help being us. Help being what we are.
Angela Which is?
Beverly No good at anything and a bit useless. Take me. Does anybody think I'll ever be a dancer—I mean a proper dancer?

A silence

You've got to be properly trained to start with and I haven't had any training at all. I've never been given the chance. But even if I had, I probably wouldn't have taken it. Because I'm too lazy, that's why. Just look at what I've done in school. Nothing. Just wasted my time for five years, messing about, trying to do maths, and not able to, trying to write essays and not able to, trying this and that—I can't even sew things together very well, or even cook things—after five years! I can't dance. I only wish I could dance, that's all. I'll never be a dancer. Never.
Fiona But you will, Bev, I know you will if you keep trying.
Beverly Never. And you'll never be a nurse because—well, it doesn't matter.
Fiona Why?
Beverly Because you're like me—you're not intelligent enough.
Fiona I am. I could be. I . . .
Beverly You're "E" Stream like me—like all of us here.
Fiona That doesn't mean anything—really . . .
Beverly And you, Mandy, won't ever be an air hostess. And Angela—you won't ever be a model. And Joan—you . . . (*She hesitates*)
Joan All I ever wanted was to be happily married, that's all.

Ever since I was a little girl that's all I ever dreamed of. I used to play being a mother—and now everything's gone wrong.

Mandy But everything will be all right, I'm sure it will, Joan. It has to be. You have to believe it will be all right, Joan.

Beverly Nothing will. Never. Not for us. We just wait here to go in there and see about a job and there won't be anything any good we can do.

Angela All they'll offer us will be the nothing jobs.

Fiona But it'll be all right in the end. Things will work out all right in the end.

Joan I don't feel very well. I feel sick.

Fiona But things will, I know they will, I'm sure they will.

Mandy They have to. I won't take any job. I won't work in a shop serving behind the counter or anything. I couldn't do it, I just couldn't.

Angela The last time I was here they said they could find me a job in a warehouse.

Beverly And they said I could get a job in a supermarket.

Fiona They said there was nothing for me and for me to come back.

Mandy But things must work out all right in the end.

Joan I feel sick.

CURTAIN

FURNITURE AND PROPERTY LIST

On stage: 6 upright chairs

Personal: **Angela**: nail file, chewing-gum

LIGHTING PLOT

Property fittings required: nil
A waiting-room

To open:	Overall rather cold, hard lighting	
Cue 1	As **Angela** and **Beverly** begin to dance *Lights change colours, spotted lights flash, to give dance floor effect. Continue until dance ends, then revert to normal lighting*	(Page 5)
Cue 2	**Girls** make noise of aeroplane engines *Gradual change of lighting to simulate aeroplane cabin*	(Page 7)
Cue 3	**Fiona**: "When we land, please." *Revert to normal lighting*	(Page 8)
Cue 4	**Fiona**: "And doctors." *Lighting change to suggest hospital operating theatre*	(Page 10)
Cue 5	**Fiona**: ". . . let me see—bed-pan." *Revert to normal lighting*	(Page 11)
Cue 6	**Beverly**: "Here we have Angela . . ." *Change to soft, "fashion parade" lighting*	(Page 12)
Cue 7	**Fiona**: "What have I done now?" *Revert to normal lighting*	(Page 13)

EFFECTS PLOT

Cue 1	As **Angela** and **Beverly** begin to dance *Dance music—gradually increasing in volume. Continue until dance ends*	(Page 5)
Cue 2	**Girls** make noise of aeroplane engines *Fade in sound of real aeroplane engines—loud, then slightly fading as dialogue starts*	(Page 7)
Cue 3	**Fiona**: "When we land, please." *Fade aeroplane engines*	(Page 8)
Cue 4	**Fiona**: "And doctors." *Music—signature tune of TV hospital series, followed by ambulance siren*	(Page 10)
Cue 5	**Beverly**: "Here we have Angela . . ." *Sweet music for "fashion parade"*	(Page 12)
Cue 6	**Fiona**: "What have I done now?" *Music stops*	(Page 13)

Sound effects on record and cassette are available from Samuel French Ltd.

Printed by The Kingfisher Press, London NW10 7AS